LIA CHANG

DEREK WALCOTT

MOON-CHILD

Derek Walcott was born in St. Lucia in 1930. He is the author
of fourteen collections of poetry, a book of essays, and many
plays. He received the Nobel Prize in Literature in 1992.

ALSO BY DEREK WALCOTT

PLAYS

Dream on Monkey Mountain and Other Plays

The Joker of Seville and O Babylon!

Remembrance and Pantomime

Three Plays: The Last Carnival; Beef, No Chicken; Branch of the Blue Nile

The Odyssey

The Haitian Trilogy

Walker and The Ghost Dance

POEMS

In a Green Night: Poems 1948–1960

The Castaway and Other Poems

The Gulf and Other Poems

Another Life

Sea Grapes

The Star-Apple Kingdom

The Fortunate Traveller

Midsummer

Collected Poems: 1948–1984

The Arkansas Testament

Omeros

The Bounty

Tiepolo's Hound

The Prodigal

Selected Poems

White Egrets

ESSAYS

What the Twilight Says

MOON-CHILD

MOON-CHILD

A PLAY

DEREK WALCOTT

ARRAR, STRAUS AND GIROU

NEW YORK

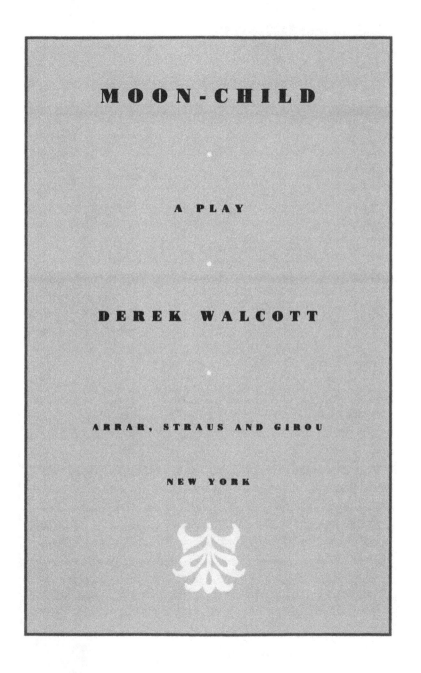

Farrar, Straus and Giroux
18 West 18th Street, New York 10011

Copyright © 2012 by Derek Walcott
Distributed in Canada by D&M Publishers, Inc.
First edition, 2012

Library of Congress Cataloging-in-Publication Data
Walcott, Derek.
    Moon-child : a play / Derek Walcott. — 1st ed.
      p.   cm.
    ISBN 978-0-374-53339-7
    I. Title.

PR9272.9.W3 M66 2012
812'.54—dc23

                                                    2011041205

Designed by Abby Kagan

www.fsgbooks.com

P1

For Sigrid

For a tear is an intellectual thing.

—WILLIAM BLAKE

MOON-CHILD

Moon-Child premiered at the American Academy in Rome on April 4, 2011, with the following cast:

The Planter	Wendell Manwarren
The Mother	Giovanna Bozzolo
The Bolom	Dean Atta
Narrator	Derek Walcott

Directed by Derek Walcott

It was produced at the Lakeside Theatre at the University of Essex on April 30, 2011, with the following cast:

The Planter	Wendell Manwarren
The Mother	Lesley-Anne Wells
The Bolom	Dean Atta
Narrator	Glyn Maxwell

Directed by Derek Walcott

CAST (IN ORDER OF APPEARANCE)

THE MOTHER

WASHERWOMEN (CHORUS)

NARRATOR

TI-JEAN

BETTY FAY (FIREFLY)

MISS MERLE (BLACKBIRD)

CUSTOMERS (CHORUS)

M. CRAPAUD (TOAD)

M. CRICHETTE (CRICKET)

THE BOLOM

ORCHESTRA

GROS-JEAN

PAPA BOIS

GUESTS (CHORUS)

THE LOUPGAROU (WEREWOLF)

MAMAN DE L'EAU

THE WHITE OWL (OWL WOMAN)

THE PLANTER

FELIX PROSPÈRE

CAST (IN ORDER OF APPEARANCE)

MI-JEAN

THE GOAT

IMPS (CHORUS)

BACKUP GIRLS (CHORUS)

LABOURERS (CHORUS)

I

PROLOGUE

[THE MOTHER *and* WASHERWOMEN,
washing by the river stones.]

THE MOTHER

If you tell me "You lie!" you
can trust me, I'll understand;
that man pulling a canoe
on the cold morning sand
at Bouton with one hand
was Alcindor, my husband,
Soufrière born and bred.
Is twelve years since he dead.
His back broad as the laurel,
we never never quarrel.
I lie! We quarrel once.

WASHERWOMEN

The white stones by the river—
Every one of them believe her

THE MOTHER

A man of good reasoning,
He leave me with three sons.
He was my daily bread,
my salt, my seasoning.
I miss him as dry season
in March missing the rain;
men so don't come again.
Everything does pass, even pain.
In early, early morning
when the stuttering candle
of the morning star go out,
I have so much to handle,
so much to think about,
I wish that every bundle
of washing was his shirt.

WASHERWOMEN

The white stones by the river—
Every one of them believe her.

[*Exit.*]

ONE

[*A full moon over Soufrière.* FELIX PROSPÈRE*'s
cabaret. A corner near the window.* NARRATOR
enters, sits at a small table.]

NARRATOR

Set in a ring of mountains
in sulphurous blue air,
a church tower and its fountain's
dry mouth say "Soufrière."
When woodsmoke climbs the valley
and immortelles catch flame,
blackbirds shoot in a volley
if you should shout his name.

[*Stands, shouts.*]

"Ti-Jean, Ti-Jean, oy!"

TI-JEAN'S VOICE
[*Distant.*]

Ayti?
Yes?

NARRATOR

Ous la' toujours?
You still there?

TI-JEAN
[*Distant.*]

Toujours!

NARRATOR

The coiled ear hears the call
of the sea curled in a shell;
boys' cries in a waterfall,
a twittering *ci-ci merle*;
now the whole island smells
like cake left in an oven
as the tower lifts its bell's
jubilate to heaven.

A time when none must quarrel,
season of love and peace;
of ham with clove and sorrel,
black pudding, *pain épice.*

When a breeze, cool and fragrant,
we call the Christmas wind
to *malheureux* and vagrant
is charitable and kind.

           [*Sounds of a rainy night.*]

That Christmas in Soufrière,
they meet in the cabaret
belonging to Felix Prospère;
Tomorrow is Boxing Day
with imps and drums and fife;
the Devil will act his play
of the Resurrection and the Life.

The night is pelting rain,
the sky: electric danger,
water races in each drain,

           [*Horse's hooves.*]

and the rain brings a stranger.

     [*A horse's whinny. Thunder.* BETTY FAY *enters.*]

A firefly starts and stops,
her name is Betty Fay;
she darts between raindrops
to the bright cabaret.
You can't see the Piton,
it's hiding in a cloud,
as Miss Merle, sable musician,
mesmerizes the crowd

inside Prospère's rum shop—
a candle on each table—
the blackbird cannot stop
singing its famous fable.

The blackbird with her yodel
is bringing down the place
with the cricket playing fiddle
and the bullfrog pulling bass.
The story she will tell you
is better in Creole.
It was when there was a Devil
and you could see the soul.

MISS MERLE

[*Singing.*]

WHO MAKE THE DEVIL CRY?

CUSTOMERS

TI-JEAN!

MISS MERLE

BRING WATER TO HIS EYE?

CUSTOMERS

TI-JEAN!

MISS MERLE

WHOSE STORY NEVER DIE?

CUSTOMERS

TI-JEAN!

M. CRAPAUD

AND HE UP THERE IN THE MOON

MISS MERLE

AND ALL THE COUNTRY CHILDREN
SINGING THIS TUNE

CUSTOMERS

LA LA LA LA LA LA
LA LA
LA LA LA LA LA LA
LA LA

M. CRAPAUD

WHO CHALLENGE PAPA BOIS?

CUSTOMERS

TI-JEAN!

MISS MERLE

WHO SEE WHEN YOU SUFFER?

CUSTOMERS

TI-JEAN!

TI-JEAN

WHO LAUGH AT LUCIFER?

CUSTOMERS

TI-JEAN!

M. CRAPAUD

AND HE SAILING WITH THE MOON

M. CRICHETTE

AND ALL THE COUNTRY CHILDREN
SINGING THIS TUNE

MISS MERLE

NOW THE *GENS-GAGÉ* WALKING
MAMAN DE L'EAU START TO SWIM
LITTLE BOLOM START TALKING
BUT YOU CAN'T TALK BACK TO HIM
YOU CAN'T TALK BACK TO HIM
NOW THE LOUPGAROU HIDING
IN THE USUAL PLACE
WHEN THE SMALL OWL START BRIGHTENING
THE TWO MOONS IN HER FACE

CUSTOMERS

THE TWO MOONS IN HER FACE

MISS MERLE

WHO MAKE THE CRICKET SING?

CUSTOMERS

TI-JEAN!

M. CRAPAUD

WHO CROWN THE CRAPAUD KING?

CUSTOMERS

TI-JEAN!

M. CRAPAUD

AND HE HAPPY AS THE MOON
AND ALL THE COUNTRY CHILDREN
SINGING THIS TUNE

CUSTOMERS

LA LA LA LA LA LA
LA LA
LA LA LA LA LA LA
LA LA

[*Music, singing, fade.*]

NARRATOR

Dawn parts the cloud's curtains,
the island is still sleeping,
between her two bare mountains
the horned moon is peeping
out of a dewy grove;
you hear the gentle throttle
of a vibrating dove
like a boy blowing a bottle.

Dawn. Far out to sea.
Look! dolphins playing
like rainbows arching,
first drizzling shafts, then rain
with its loud lances marching;
at smoke-rise, mysteries,
from a sunlit country road
smelling of hog-plum and the sea's
remembered boyhood.

The light from Bouton on the sea
is a breath-stopping view
of sunlit slopes whose honesty
will break your heart in two.
At dusk the sea pulls in its ropes,
canoes are coming home:

the names of fishermen whose hopes
are muttered by the foam.
Places like this, people have said,
should still be left alone.
All the best views have been surveyed
and soon they could be gone.

Above the herringboned bay
a scissor-tailed frigate sails;
there'll be a great catch today.
Balahoo will tilt the scales;
dorado, grouper, and *demoiselles*
and flying fish'll fill the basket,
while the black stingray fills
that canoe like its casket.
It is the fish of death,
of fear and superstition,
nasty its reeking breath,
sweeping and wide its mission.

The night is full of noises,
the country people say;
the moonlit leaves have voices,
loupgarou, gens-gagé,
dovens, but where precisely
is this wild creature from,

a voice that sings so nicely,
who answers to "*Beau l'homme*"?
An apparition scary
behind its gum-sealed eyes,
the Devil's emissary
who brings his messages.

In moonlight, walk with caution
on the bright country road
and you'll meet this abortion
hopping there like a toad,
hopping with feet reversed
still unbaptised, still cursed,
crawling between two worlds, this
and the world to come,
a caul around its hump, this
miscarriage from Time's womb.
            [*Sound of wind and rain. A piercing fife.*]
Through sheeted gusts of rain
curling like a dead leaf,
rolled in a scroll of pain,
this messenger of grief,
through drum-bursts in the clouds
and the wind whipping wild
and the sky's tattered shrouds
she hears a shrieking child;
in her African belief.

THE BOLOM

Listen! The Devil, my master,
who owns half the world,
still cannot enjoy
those vices he created.
He is dying to be human.
So he sends you this challenge!
To all three of your sons,
he says, through my voice,
that if any one of them
can make him feel anger,
rage, or human weakness,
he will reward him,
he will fill that bowl
with a shower of sovereigns,
you shall never more know hunger,
but fulfillment, wealth, peace.

But if any of your sons
fails to give him these feelings—
for he never was human—
then his flesh shall be eaten,
for he is weary of the flesh
of the fowls of the air
and the fishes of the sea.
But whichever of your sons
is brave enough to do this,

then that one shall inherit

the wealth of my prince.

And once they are dead, woman,

I too shall feel life!

I shall feel life.

[*Exterior.* THE BOLOM *withdraws into the leaves,*
singing. The full moon sails on.]

[*Singing.*]

OH, ME WANT TO GO OVER

YES, MAMAN, ME WANT TO GO OVER . . .

M. CRAPAUD AND ORCHESTRA

OH, ME WANT TO GO OVER

YES, MAMAN, ME WANT TO GO OVER . . .

[CUSTOMERS *sing.*]

CUSTOMERS

OH, ME WANT TO GO OVER . . .

[*Fade.*]

[*Exterior. Sunrise, the heights. A* B L A C K B I R D *twitters, a* T O A D *booms and belches, a* C R I C K E T *chafes its legs, rattling.*]

NARRATOR

How fresh is the sweet morning
above benign Bouton!
Despite the Bolom's warning
Gros-Jean will leave at dawn;
he sees his weeping mother's
goodbye of streaming tears
but does not tell his brothers.
He is the first in years;
she sees him climb the small track
up from the house; her fears
rise as she hears him sing.

THE BOLOM

"Your son is
not coming back!"

NARRATOR

The gliricidia's boughs
are trembling in the light,
the path above the house,
cool in the mountain height,
they are good boundary trees,
they grip earth round a boulder.
His song rides on the breeze,
the axe slung on his shoulder;
he hears the steady rattle
made by a parched cicada;
it's deafening, but that'll
only make him march the harder.
Dawn breaks over Bouton
while Gros-Jean, carefully,
eases the latch where she
sleeps in the shuttered house.

GROS-JEAN

[*Singing.*]

THERE'S A TIME FOR EVERY MAN
TO LEAVE HIS MOTHER AND FATHER
TO LEAVE EVERYBODY HE KNOW
AND MARCH TO THE GRAVE, HE ONE!
HE ONE
AND MARCH TO THE GRAVE, HE ONE

SO THE TIME HAS COME FOR ME
TO LEAVE MY POOR LITTLE MOTHER
TO LEAVE ME TWO OTHER BROTHER
AND MARCH TO THE GRAVE, ME ONE
AND MARCH TO THE GRAVE, ME ONE

WASHERWOMEN
SO THE TIME HAS COME FOR HIM
TO LEAVE HIS POOR LITTLE MOTHER
TO LEAVE HIS TWO OTHER BROTHER
AND MARCH TO THE GRAVE, HE ONE
AND MARCH TO THE GRAVE, HE ONE

GROS-JEAN
I HAVE AN ARM OF IRON

WASHERWOMEN
ARM OF IRON

NARRATOR
Climbing up through the forest
he passed trees that he knew,
bois-canot, cedar, the blest
laurier-canelles, acajou;
those ferns that shut their eyes
like maidens from a touch,
the spears of paradise:

the *balisier*'s bright torch,
all of the ripe wild fruits
that shake loose to the pound
of Gros-Jean's yellow boots
on the ant-crazy ground.

GROS-JEAN

[*Singing.*]

I HAVE AN ARM OF IRON

WASHERWOMEN

ARM OF IRON

GROS-JEAN

I COME OUT TO WORK

WASHERWOMEN

COME OUT TO WORK

GROS-JEAN

GIVE ME SERIOUS LABOUR

WASHERWOMEN

SERIOUS LABOUR

GROS-JEAN

THIS WORK IS A JOKE

WASHERWOMEN

THIS WORK IS A JOKE

[PAPA BOIS *emerges from the bush.*]

NARRATOR

Deep in the forest, thick,
where precious creatures are:
the dove, the emerald, electric
hummingbird, old as Noah,
is the wild man, Papa Bois.
A legendary creature
like Noah and the ark,
tree-like in every feature,
his face as rough as bark.
Like two coals his red eyes,
his hair like brown lianas,
his beard cotton, his hands nimble as butterflies.

PAPA BOIS

Good morning. You have no manners?

GROS-JEAN

Who is you?

PAPA BOIS

I heard a rustle in the grass
but first, you swear obedience,
then Papa Bois will let you pass,
at least for just this once.

GROS-JEAN

I don't swear. I don't curse.

NARRATOR

His shirt of dry banana fronds
kept rattling from the wind,
his brow, with two capricious horns,
had mischief on its mind;
his breath, its reek could stifle;
he kept, slung from his waist,
a rusty flintlock rifle
with his archaic taste,
the dog-head snake, the iron lance,
like pets coiled round his hands.

PAPA BOIS

For fifty years I have lived here,
just listen and I'll tell you,
as horned and careful as the deer
I sniff the air and smell you.
I am, if you believe in me,

the prophet of protection,
the bush is my constituency;
I don't need no election.
I have my signals and alarms
when hunters stalk my forest,
the angry trees will shake their arms
and birds will scream their loudest.

[*Birds scream.*]

My cannon is my thunder,
the red ant is my nation,
their armies all come under
my daily domination.
The marching termites carry
their leaf-flags in battalions,
their dead the spiders bury
with beetles in alliance.
The hummingbird's helicopter
drills nectar from the flowers
and nobody has ever stopped the
bat's acrobatic powers.
I lose a little every day,
my forces, my militia,
but let them guard you on your way—
the good day I wish you.
What is your name, you say?

GROS-JEAN
[*Growling.*]

GROS-JEAN!

MISS MERLE
[*Singing.*]
PAPA BOIS, WHAT YOU COOK TODAY?

PAPA BOIS
[*Singing.*]
SWEET POTATO AND *BOIS BANDÉ*

M. CRAPAUD
PAPA BOIS, PAPA BOIS, WHAT YOU COOK TODAY?

PAPA BOIS
DASHEEN, *TANIA*, AND *BOIS BANDÉ*
I LOVE THESE GREEN BANANAS
MACAMBU AND SALTFISH
I'LL PUT YOU ON MY HEAVY MANNERS
IF YOU DEFY MY WISH
DON'T KICK THE LIFE FROM YOUR BROTHER
[*A grunt.*]

M. CRAPAUD
UNH!

DEREK WALCOTT

PAPA BOIS

AND DO NOT STONE THE BIRD

MISS MERLE
[Shrieks.]

E.E.E.E.GAS!

M. CRICHETTE

"MEN MUST LOVE ONE ANOTHER"

PAPA BOIS

LET PAPA BOIS BE HEARD
THE LIZARD, THE AGOUTI
THE MOTH WITH EYES FOR WINGS
ARE ONE IN NATURE'S BEAUTY
HEAR WHAT THE BLACKBIRD SINGS

NARRATOR

The names that we are given
are who we will become:
"Satan" can't live in heaven
and "hell" sounds like his home.
So there were names for each son:
big, medium, and small.
Gros-Jean, Mi-Jean, and Ti-Jean
will answer if you call.

Some tall men are called *Shorty*!
The nickname passes on.
Some big men over forty
will answer to GARÇON!

But Gros-Jean couldn't take it
if you forgot his name.
What difference did it make if
black people looked the same?
The Planter called him Hubert,
Theophilius, Max, and Joe;
not one of them was true, but
how could the Planter know?
To him they all resembled
each other on paydays;
at three when they assembled
any name fit the face.

PAPA BOIS

You are a man of iron
or so, at least, you claim
and you roar like a lion
if men forget your name.
I only try to warn you,
beware the aftermath;
one thing you must remember,
you must control your wrath,

you must not lose your temper,
you'll lose the strength you have.

Goodbye!

GROS-JEAN

Move! You blasted fool!

[*Exits.*]

THREE

M. CRICHETTE
[*Singing.*]
THE PLANTER GAVE A COSTUME PARTY
IN SOUFRIÈRE, A 'MAS BALL
THE APPETITE WAS HEARTY
TO WELCOME IN CARNIVAL
THE GUESTS WERE HIS RICH NEIGHBOURS
ALL OF THEM CAME IN DISGUISE
AND THE HIGHLIGHT OF GROS-JEAN'S LABOURS
WAS A BASKET OF FIREFLIES

GUESTS
WOI-WOI-MI DIABLE LA
OHO I-HO MI DIABLE LA

[*Exterior. Night. The Estate House, hung with decorations.
The driveway lit with flambeaux.* GUESTS *begin arriving,
are given masks and led up to the house. A white estate
owner—a* WEREWOLF, *or* LOUPGAROU, *mask.*

A white young woman, a MAMAN DE L'EAU *mask, flour*
white with long black hair; an aging white woman in her
soucouyant *mask, vampire teeth, huge skirts, a bandana.*
THE PLANTER *greets them.*]
HE HIRE US TO PLAY
COUNTRY MUSIC AT HIS EXPENSE
HE HAD CHAMPAGNE FOR THE *GENS-GAGÉS*
AND SWEET DRINK FOR THE LITTLE DOUENS.
[GROS-JEAN *in headwaiter's jacket.*]

M. CRICHETTE
THE LOUPGAROU SMELL SOUP
HE HAD A CHICKEN INSIDE HIS JACKET
FROM RAIDING THE CHICKEN COOP
BUT THE FOWLS MADE TOO MUCH RACKET
HIS ESCORT WAS MAMAN DE L'EAU
AND THE PRESENT THAT HE GAVE HER
TO WEAR TO THIS DINNER SHOW
WAS A DEAD RAT FROM THE RIVER

GUESTS
WOI-WOI-MI DIABLE LA
OHO I-HO MI DIABLE LA
[*Interior. The Estate House.* GROS-JEAN *ripping*
at his bow tie in the bathroom and cursing. He goes through
the spinning door, balancing a tray.]

THE PLANTER

How good to see you, how very very good,
to come to my little place! Welcome!
In those old rafters there's a nest
where a disheveled owl
rattles dead rats in its beak.
Are you Gros-Islet?

GROS-JEAN

[*Grinding his teeth, then grinning.*]

No. Gros-Islet is a town. I am not a town.

THE PLANTER

You're big enough.

THE LOUPGAROU

[*Seated at a table.*]

Waiter! Over here!

MAMAN DE L'EAU

Waiter! *Garçon!*

THE WHITE OWL

Boy!

THE PLANTER

That would be you.

[GROS-JEAN *goes over to* THE LOUPGAROU.]

THE LOUPGAROU

Do you have any pepper sauce?

GROS-JEAN

Please? Sir, say please!
If you don't mind.

[THE PLANTER *comes over.*]

THE PLANTER

Just serve the damned sauce, will you, Stanley!

GROS-JEAN

Look! *Gadez!* I is a big man with an iron arm
and I not used to smiling service.
I try hard not to lose my temper
but you pushing me, you really pushing me!
That is not nice.

[GROS-JEAN *is serving with two maids.*]

THE PLANTER

Service, Walter, service!

GROS-JEAN

Sir, I don't like . . .

THE PLANTER

Hospitality, hospitality!
That's the future of this island!
My future is yours. So never get vex.
How often do guests eat the orchestra?

GROS-JEAN

Sir, may I speak a word with you alone?
  [GROS-JEAN *goes to a corner of the room near a painted
    screen.* THE PLANTER *comes up to him. They talk in
    whispers while smiling at the guests.*]
You know their name, but you ain't know mine?
I work for you, you never notice?

THE PLANTER

I know your name, it's . . . it's just slipped me.
I should have given you a tag with your name, George.

GROS-JEAN

Not George. Gros . . .
        [*Interior.* THE PLANTER *'s dining room.*]

FELIX PROSPÈRE

I don't eat crickets.
Moi pas ka manger crichettes.

THE PLANTER

Also on our local, succulent list—
ramier, a plump, mellifluous bird
also known as ortolan, crunchy
when done to a crisp and nimbler,
the little warbler can be heard in the cedars
twittering her plaintive prayers.
The dry cicada is a dessert dish
like that precisely! Some cultures
find the cricket or grasshopper a crisp,
delicate item succulent with honey.

FELIX PROSPÈRE

My English is not so good . . .
               [*Reads his card. Singing.*]
A DEALER IN RETAIL, A MERCHANT
OF SALTFISH, KEROSENE, RICE
I PROFIT IN PENNIES YOU CAN'T
GO WRONG IF YOU JACK UP THE PRICE
OF SALT PORK, EGGS, AND SMALL ONIONS
NOW I'LL TELL YOU SOMETHING FUNNY
TAKE MY EXPERIENCED ADVICE
POOR PEOPLE WILL ALWAYS FIND MONEY

TO EAT BECAUSE HUNGRY. NOT NICE
A TOAST TO YOU, MY COMPANIONS
IN ONIONS AND AVARICE

[*Applause.*]

THE PLANTER

Wonderful. Now you, Cousin Louise.

THE WHITE OWL

I WEAR THE MASK OF AN OWL
BECAUSE IT CONCEALS MY SOUL

[*Silence.*]

THE LOUPGAROU

That's all?

[*Silence.*]

THE SOUCOUYANT

That says everything.

THE PLANTER

Now, ladies, gentlemen, and creatures,
if you will please peruse your menus.
Frog's leg soup. A speciality
of our neighbouring island, Dominica.
Now, Lou, will you begin?

[*Tinkles the bell.*]

[THE LOUPGAROU *wears the wolf mask. We hear a hunting horn and yelping dogs.*]

THE LOUPGAROU

[*Reads his dinner card.*]

NEITHER THE SOUND OF THE HORN
NOR THE PANTING DOGS OF THE CHASE
CAN CATCH ME. I WAS BORN
FAST AND RAVENOUS, WITH THE STENCH
OF A WOLF. MY ORIGIN IS FRENCH.
I AM DOING WHAT YOU ASK
BUT NO MASK CAN HIDE MY VICE—
MY VULPINE AVARICE

What does it mean, "vulpine"?

THE PLANTER

"Vulpine"? Overcharging poor people,
like we all do.
Your turn, Maman de L'Eau.

MAMAN DE L'EAU

[*Reads her card. Singing.*]

ONE TOUCH OF THE SCORCHING SUN
CAN RUIN MY COMPLEXION
I AM THE SKY-ARC'S DAUGHTER
MY ELEMENT IS WATER
MY TEETH TEAR FISH TO THE BONES

MY SHADOW GLIDES OVER THE STONES
[*Applause.*]

THE PLANTER
[*Tinkles the bell.*]

Let's go on.

THE LOUPGAROU

When I look in the mirror
I frighten myself sometimes.
There is no reflection.
Should a werewolf
part his hair in the center?

MAMAN DE L'EAU

People here are so superstitious!
I go in the waterfall some mornings
and sometimes when boys are bathing
and I put on a white sunscreen for the sun,
it sends them screaming in a frenzy of desire.
It's the fury of puberty, but desire all the same.

THE PLANTER

People will see what they believe.
They believe in spirits because they need to.
[*To* GROS-JEAN.]
You agree, Cuthbert?

GROS-JEAN
[*Grinning.*]
I am not Cuthbert, sir.

THE PLANTER
You know, people think I'm the archfiend.

THE LOUPGAROU
They're just jealous of your money.

THE WHITE OWL
And your complexion.
[*Pause.*]
And your accent.
[*Pause.*]

FELIX PROSPÈRE
And your education.

THE PLANTER
I'm teaching Morris here,
but don't worry, ladies,
he won't drop the soup.
We're celebrating the sale of Prospère's property,
I've chosen the best orchestra
to serenade your savours and a menu.
Instead of us old estate owners,

we have corporations now,
but predators all the same.
This is sort of a farewell dinner
because we are a dying breed,
we incestuous Creoles,
are we not, Cousin Louise?

THE WHITE OWL

I've never committed incest,
not intentionally, anyway.

THE PLANTER

You have a short memory, dear.

THE WHITE OWL

Well, we were children then, cousin.
                    [*They sit in their places.*]

THE PLANTER

Now, are we all seated?
This may be a trifle blasphemous,
but I am going to play priest
with this little bell, signaling
the hoisting of the host or something:
your confession, before we break bread.
Ladies and monsters! The main item on the menu!
Smile, Gros Negre, smile and serve!

GROS-JEAN

I not vex, chief. Look! I smiling.

I not vex, see? Big smile!

[THE PLANTER *advances towards*

GROS-JEAN.]

THE PLANTER

[*Shouts.*]

BAI DIABLE LA MANGER UN' TI MAMAI

GIVE THE DEVIL A CHILD FOR DINNER

GUESTS

ONE!

M. CRAPAUD

We all know Gros-Jean's evil

was his bad temper, NEXT!

You cannot beat the Devil.

You shouldn't get so vexed. NEXT!

[*An explosion.* GROS-JEAN*'s axe and hat*

sail onto the stage.]

THE PLANTER

Bai Diable—la manger un' ti mamai!

One!

II

Now for the second son,
they were calling him Mi-Jean.
Nobody was happier
with deeds and litigation
than this *avocat 'ti papier*
with prestidigitation
and with no legal basis
handling *chou-maman* cases,
claiming he was well-read
in jurisprudent talk,
papers flying round his head
like sea birds round a rock.

MI-JEAN
[*Singing.*]

IF I WAS A WHITE MAN
AND WAS VERY RICH
I WOULD LEAVE THIS COUNTRY
QUICK QUICK QUICK
CAUSE THE WAY THINGS ARE GOING
IT WOULDN'T BE LONG

BEFORE SOME BIG NIGGER
TAKE A BIG STICK AND KNOCK ME DOWN

M. CRAPAUD AND M. CRICHETTE AND
MISS MERLE
[*Singing.*]

IF HE WAS A WHITE MAN
AND WAS VERY RICH
HE WOULD LEAVE THIS COUNTRY
QUICK QUICK QUICK
CAUSE THE WAY THINGS ARE GOING
IT WOULDN'T BE LONG
BEFORE SOME BIG NIGGER
TAKE A BIG STICK AND KNOCK HIM DOWN

NARRATOR

All lawyers are loquacious.
Mi-Jean believed that one
of his most sagacious
strategies was to play dumb;
if discussion got heated,
then silence meant contempt,
he could not be defeated
without an argument.
He wouldn't indulge the Planter.
It wasn't worth the while

to cite question and answer,
nod "yes" or "no," but smile.

MI-JEAN

[*Singing.*]

WITHIN THE BOOK OF WISDOM
HEAR WHAT THE WISE MAN SAY
THE MAN WHO IS WISE IS DUMB
AND LIVES ANOTHER DAY
YOU CANNOT BEAT THE SYSTEM
DEBATE IS JUST A HOOK
OPEN YOUR MOUTH, DE BAIT IN!
AND IS YOU THEY GOING TO JUK
I READ IT IN THIS BOOK

M. CRAPAUD AND M. CRICHETTE
AND MISS MERLE

SO WHEN THINGS DARK, GO BLIND
WHEN NOTHING LEFT, GO DEAF
AND WHEN THE BLOWS COME, BE DUMB
AND HUM HUM

MI-JEAN

IN CHAPTER FIVE FROM
PARAGRAPH THREE, PAGE 79
THIS BOOK OPINES HOW

SOCRATES WOULD HAVE BEEN BETTER OFF BLIND
GOD GAVE HIM EYES LIKE ALL WE
BUT HE, HE HAD TO LOOK
THE NEXT THING, FRIENDS, WAS JAIL, *OUI*!
HEMLOCK AND HIM LOCK UP!

M. CRAPAUD AND M. CRICHETTE

AND MISS MERLE

SO WHEN THINGS DARK, GO BLIND
WHEN NOTHING LEFT, GO DEAF
AND WHEN THE BLOWS COME, BE DUMB
AND HUM HUM

MI-JEAN

THE THIRD SET OF INSTRUCTION
THIS SELF-SAID BOOK DECLARES
IS THAT THE WISE MAN'S FUNCTION
IS HOW TO SHUT HIS EARS
AGAINST RIOT AND RUCTION
THAT TRY TO CLIMB UPSTAIRS
IF YOU CAN HEAR, DON'T LISTEN!
IF YOU MUST TALK, BE QUIET!
OR YOUR MOUTH WILL DIG YOUR GRAVE

LA LA LA LA LA LA
LA LA LA LA LA
LA LA LA LA LA

NARRATOR

Pride is the great destroyer
and it is Mi-Jean's boast
that he's the smartest lawyer
along the leeward coast.
Confident of victory,
he never went to court,
knowing his triumph would be
not in muscle but in thought.
From here we see the sequel:
the cunning of the Planter
was to treat him like an equal
in question and in answer,
but little did he know that
he should have taken note
since his opposing *avocat*
was *un cabrit*, a goat.

MI-JEAN

A goat?

THE GOAT
[*Bleats.*]
Yeah, goat. That's right. G.O.T.E.

THE PLANTER

Did you catch the wild goat?

[*He sits on a log, legs crossed, smiling through the scene.*]

Did you tie him?

[MI-JEAN *nods.*]

Frisky little bugger, wasn't he?

[MI-JEAN *nods.*]

Look, you don't mind a little chat while we work, do you?
Where did you get your reputation as a bush lawyer? I mean,
it's only manners, damn it.

[THE GOAT *bleats repeatedly.*]

MI-JEAN

That capriped certainly making a plethora of cacophony.

THE PLANTER

It's only a poor animal, in its own rut. Let's take a salubrious
stroll to the volcano.

[*Exterior. They begin walking.*]

MI-JEAN

Men are lustiferous animals also, but at least they have souls.

THE PLANTER

Ah, a philosopher! A contemplative! A man is not better than
an animal. The one with two legs makes more noise and that

makes him believe he can think. It is talk that makes men think they have souls. There is no difference, only in degree. No animal but man, dear boy, savours such a variety of vices. He knows no season for lust, he is a kneeling hypocrite who, on four legs like a penitent capriped, prays to his maker but is calculating the next vice. That's my case!

MI-JEAN

Nonsensical verbiage! *Bêtise!*

THE PLANTER

It's not, you know, and you're getting annoyed. Oh, I hear him bleating. We have to go back.

MI-JEAN
[*Shakes his head.*]

You can't get me into an argument! I have brains, but I won't talk.
[*Long pause.*]
All I say is, that man is divine!

THE GOAT
[*Far off.*]

Gimme a break!

MI-JEAN

Did that illiterate quadruped say

[*In American.*]

"Gimme a break?"

[*They get nearer to the house.*]

THE PLANTER

You're more intelligent than the goat, you think?

MI-JEAN

I not arguing! Anything you want.

THE GOAT

Good move, bonehead! Yeaah!

THE PLANTER

The Greek word for tragedy is "goat-song."

[MI-JEAN *rising, about to lecture.* THE GOAT *bleats.*]

For all we know, that may be poetry. Which Greek scholar contends, in his theory of metempsychosis, that the souls of men may return in animals?

MI-JEAN

I never study Greek, but I . . .

[THE GOAT *bleats.* MI-JEAN *pauses.*]

I was saying that I never study no Greek, but I'd . . .

[THE GOAT *bleats.*]

It getting on like it have sense, eh?

[*To* THE GOAT.]

Paix chou-ous, cabrit!

Grand n'hommes ka parler!

Shut your backside, goat!

Big men talking!

THE PLANTER

Why not? A sensible goat?

THE GOAT

Yeah. Why not?

MI-JEAN

Listen, I ent mind doing what you proposed. Anything phys-
ical, because that's ostentatious, but when you start theoriz-
ing that there's an equality of importance in the creatures of
this earth, when you animadvertently imbue mere animals
with an animus or soul, I have to call you a crooked-minded
pantheist.

[THE GOAT *bleats, sounding like "Hear hear!"*]

Oh shut up, you can't hear two people talking? No, I'm not
vexed, you know, but . . .

[THE GOAT *bleats.*]

THE PLANTER

[*Advancing towards him.*]

Your argument interests me. It's nice to see how ideas get you excited. But logically now. The goat, I contend, may be a genius in its own right. For all we know, this may be the supreme goat, the apogee of capripeds, the voice of human tragedy, the Greek . . .

MI-JEAN

Exaggerated hypothesis! Unsubstantiated!

THE PLANTER

Since the goat is mine, and if you allow me, for argument's sake, to pursue my premise, then if you get vexed at the goat, who represents my view, you are vexed with me, and the contract must be fulfilled.

MI-JEAN

I don't mind talking to you, but don't insult me, telling me a goat have more sense than I, than me. Than both of we!

[THE GOAT *sustains its bleating in furious gibberish.*]

Oh, shut you damn mouth, both o'all you! I ain't care who right or wrong! I talking now! What you ever study I ain't even finish making my points and all two of you interrupting, breach of legal practice! Oh God, I not vex, I not vex . . . *M'as facheux . . . M'as facheux!*

[THE GOAT *bleats once.*]

NARRATOR

We know that Mi-Jean's evil
was arguing, that's true,
but we all know that the Devil
can argue more than you.

THE PLANTER

Bai Diable—la manger un' ti mamai!
[*Explosion.*]

GUESTS

Deux!

THE PLANTER

Give the Devil a child for dinner!

GUESTS

Two!

THE GOAT

Yeah! All right.
[*Masquerade music. Blackout.*]
[*Fade in.*]

NARRATOR

The Planter's character,
his nature, his repute,

was of a cat-eyed actor
whose smile concealed a brute;
whose accent, inherited
from an English father, made,
although its source was dead,
for more obedience,
or so the Planter said.

THE PLANTER

I grew up as a little
copper-haired urchin diving
for pennies in green crystal
water for a living.
When dusk came I studied
under a sodium street-
lamp till my eyes were red.
There wasn't much to eat,
but by a succession of straight
A's I sailed through college
in an amazing feat,
a scholarship fed by rage.

I saw all of the great
cities of Europe, I learnt
their language, I played
their sports. Midsummer burnt

me, I skied down immaculate
slopes, but I grew homesick
for my infernal climate,
its forests, its falls, its electric
hummingbirds, their primal state.
Then my white father died,
who, from guilt, left me an immense
estate and with it the pride
that corrupts innocence.

NARRATOR

Proud, illegitimate,
prancing on his white horse,
his head aflame with hate
of his father's remorse,
and his past poverty,
the faith that told them wait
and they'd see paradise
behind its jeweled gate,
every long-suffering mother,
her slowly closing eyes
promised bliss by Another.

There her eternal hope,
that light to which she'd turn,
varnished the breezy slope

of radiant Bouton;
with faith, until at length
she sacrificed her sons
to it: Gros-Jean with his strength,
Mi-Jean, and now Ti-Jean.
The poor people were sure
he was the Devil, what was true
was: the land belonged to her
and that was all she knew.

Some spoke of him with humour
but many with belief,
some felt more fact than rumour
with superstitious grief;
some servant had surprised him
in candle-kneeling prayer,
a mask meant to disguise him
with flour-face and red hair;
with a low growl he called "Come"
in that blood-dribbling mask
to *loupgarou, gagé, bolom*
and their usual task.

Wherever his shadow passed, it
made a consternation,
a bamboo that was tacit
would burst in conflagration;

the Fire Brigade would find it
set by his central ember
that often left behind it
acres of smouldering umber,
or like two coals set in the eyes
of a marauding panther,
a *loupgarou* that was the size
of a nocturnal Planter.

THE PLANTER

Nobody dared to sue me—
you'd have to be a fool—
big businessmen would woo me,
I was too powerful.
A man of my position
had friends in Cabinet,
black, local, this one
slithered from the Law's net;
his shaven scalp as hairy
as a marble, in dark glasses,
gum-chewing, extraordinary
sleek skin, a porpoise's,
he altered boundaries.

Most of the properties'
boundaries were indistinct,
vague verbal handshakes, these

oral and never inked,
family inheritances, based on
an aunt or uncle's word,
the rim of a pond's basin,
all mental maps and blurred,
the strategy was this:
to harass the landowner
with wild nocturnal creatures . . .
the terrors that were shown her.

I had this redskin lawyer
who looked like a mongoose
with hair like copper wire
and an accountant's nose.
To him, fraud was a science;
he sifted suits and claims
and proffered deals to clients
who couldn't sign their names.
Thus lot by lot and acre
by acre the acquisitions grew
except Bouton; I'd make her
join with the others too.

Of that whole Cabinet,
three narrowly missed prison,
two more refused regret
for perjury within reason.

All were the Planter's pals
suddenly turned landowners
from deeds that were all balls,
astonishing *cojones!*
Their backsides grew as swollen
as their paunches, in dark glasses,
to colon from semicolon,
to asses from half-asses.

The dangling tarantula,
that snake, head like a dog,
that swallows chickens, tra-la-la!
comprised his catalogue;
the *sol-souris*, that flying mouse,
and the scorpion's raised question
haunted the eaves of his dark house
and no one was the best one.
Deep crevices could hide the
poison in the pearly net
of the black widow spider, also
the chattering cricket
and the bullfrog's basso.

NARRATOR

If you expected someone
haggard, sepulchral, a
hater of the sun,

with the pallor of a candle,
you would be very wrong;
he was young, supple, eager,
both serpentine and bold,
like that medieval figure
cold as a snake is cold.

His scaled skin was the colour
of Soufrière in drought,
when all its hills are ochre
and black where bush-fires caught;
the heat then is infernal,
the hot-pitch road is hell,
the white steam drifts, eternal,
from the volcano's hill
to the flames of the immortelle
and the sulphur's rotting smell.

Because his youth was tragic
and bitter from neglect
he went and studied magic
in Haiti and Tibet.
M. Prospère told people
he could see everything:
a gargoyle on a steeple
that folded its stone wing.

THE PLANTER

So in a tight medieval
city in Germany
I learnt the primal evil:
to buy men's souls for money.

Power enjoys an ecstasy
that's actual and slow,
that settles on all it can see
and smothers like the snow-
white flowers in the cedar,
embroidering the ground
with petals with as speedy
a claim and without a sound;
I saw the riotous forest
between each high Piton
and swore my soul would have no rest
until both were my own.

NARRATOR

At noon this necromancer
with a horse whip to crack
would tolerate no answer
if a labourer talked back.
For all who gave him trouble
he had a simple creed,
as simple as a stone:

that those who disagreed
with him were simply thrown
into the volcano's bubble.
They said this was well known.

Blue kitchen smoke provoking
his customers with love,
ginger-beer, sorrel soaking,
the ham studded with clove,
some black fruit cake for after,
some Martiniquan wine,
and with loud, scandalous laughter
when the Planter would wine.
For a man of such proportions
he is so light of step,
they clap at his contortions
at *piquer* and *la comette.*

Behold the Devil dancing
with step so delicate,
you'd think the weight of the world's sin
was just a feather's freight,
as if the weight of the world's grief,
the tonnage of our sin,
leapt with the lightness of a leaf
as it begins to spin,
or when a gull against the wind

buckles its wings to slide
like the long note of a violin,
sin showed the dancer's pride.

Ah fragrant, joyous season!
Ah sweet ancestral dance
that seeks no other reason
but joy in joining hands,
for hallowing the patterns
brought across the ocean,
that all the tribe knew once
the memory of motion;
goatskin and the piercing
delightful bamboo fife,
music that we can hear sing
its gratitude for life.

III

[*Bouton. Dawn.*]

NARRATOR

Now dawn comes with its heartbreak
above benign Bouton;
the mother and her last son wake
as light climbs the Piton.
The *gommier*'s flowers are arrayed
on green embroidered grass
like an altar cloth. His mother prayed:
"Hail Mary, full of grace."
From a croton bush she heard the voice
of the Bolom near her home.

THE BOLOM

My master took two of your sons,
there is the third to come.

THE MOTHER
[*Screaming.*]

Spare him!

NARRATOR

His mother screamed, but still
the flowers fell steadily
as dawn filled the golden hill.
Ti-Jean rose, readily.
Through the dawn clouds above Bouton
she watched the gold coin burn,
and then she turned and heard her son.

TI-JEAN

Maman, it is my turn.

NARRATOR

Had all the legions of the skies
in chariots of thunder
and lances of lightning laid siege
to her heart, she would not surrender
this child; this one leaf she had left
would not be shaken from her,
her widowhood bare and bereft
as a dry season *gommier.*

THE MOTHER
[*Singing.*]

IF YOU LEAVE ME, MY SON
I HAVE EMPTY HANDS LEFT
NOTHING TO GRIEVE FOR

YOU ARE HARDLY A MAN
A STALK BENDING IN THE WIND
WITH NO WILL OF ITS OWN
NEVER PROVEN YOURSELF
IN BATTLE OR IN WISDOM
I HAVE KEPT YOU TO MY BREAST
AS THE LAST OF MY CHICKENS
NOT TO FEED THE BLIND JAWS
OF THE HUNGRY GRAVE

Oh, Ti-Jean, you are so small. So small!

TI-JEAN

Yes, I small, Maman, I small,
I not strong like Gros-Jean,
not smart like Mi-Jean,
and I never learn from book,
but like the boy David,
like the small boy David.
[Singing.]
I GO BRING DOWN, BRING DOWN GOLIATH

IMPS

BRING DOWN BELOW

TI-JEAN

BRING DOWN, BRING DOWN GOLIATH

IMPS

BRING DOWN BELOW

TI-JEAN

SUNDAY MORNING I WENT TO THE CHAPEL

IMPS

BRING DOWN BELOW

TI-JEAN

I MET THE DEVIL WITH A BOOK AND A BIBLE

IMPS

BRING DOWN BELOW

TI-JEAN

ASK HIM WHAT HE WILL HAVE FOR DINNER

IMPS

BRING DOWN BELOW

TI-JEAN

CRICKET LEG AND A FROG WITH WATER

IMPS

BRING DOWN BELOW

TI-JEAN

I LEAVING HOME AND I HAVE ONE MISSION

IMPS

BRING DOWN BELOW

TI-JEAN

YOU COME TO ME BY YOUR OWN DECISION

IMPS

BRING DOWN BELOW

TI-JEAN

DOWN IN HELL YOU AWAIT YOUR VISION

IMPS

BRING DOWN BELOW

TI-JEAN

YOU WON'T GET THE LAND THAT IS MY MOTHER'S

IMPS

BRING DOWN BELOW

TI-JEAN

DO UNTO YOURSELF AS YOU DO TO OTHERS

IMPS

BRING DOWN BELOW

NARRATOR

Ti-Jean raced down a track
that could barely be seen
so he could hurry back
with a pint of kerosene;
he saw with his runaway's
eyes the African violet's
exuberant bouquets,
the acid gooseberry,
the purple governor plum,
that maiden fern, Miss Marie,
the *topis tambour*'s drum.
These fruit, they make us young,
as Ti-Jean is a boy,
bring memories to the tongue,
a feast of vanished joy;
our boyhood was the smell
of *moubain*, *pomme-arac*,
each verdant, fragrant chapel,
every leaf-sheltered well;
gooseberry, golden apple,
sung by the *ci-ci merle*.
In the waterfall's
pouring pitcher

voices of a loud dream,
as the blue kingfisher
darted and flashed upstream.

The shortcut led through many
a leaf-choked ravine
with cocoa and *shadon-beni,*
bushes and potato vine.
He raced between the bushes
with the accuracy of a bird
that arrowlike through branches
darts, until he heard
the bullfrog's abrupt answers
the tremble of the blackbird's call,
the cicada's stuttering foreword
to the hoarse waterfall.

[PAPA BOIS *enters. Sound of rustling leaves.*]

PAPA BOIS

Ah, good morning, youngster!

TI-JEAN

Good morning, sir.

PAPA BOIS

A long, long time ago
I was a hunter.

My name is Papa Bois,
father of the forest.
I found my happiness
in killing things, I shot
an agouti one sunrise,
and when I got to it,
to look death in the eye,
I saw that it was a mother.
A mother who gave birth
under the bleeding skies
on the wet morning earth.
I watch as her litter dies.
Well, after that, my boy,
my hunting days were done
from the first shafts of the sunrise
to the target of the sinking sun.
You hungry?

TI-JEAN

No thanks, sir.

MISS MERLE

PAPA BOIS, WHAT YOU COOK TODAY?

PAPA BOIS

[*Singing.*]

GOOD COUNTRY FOOD, WHAT YOU WANT ME
TO SAY?

M. CRICHETTE

Like what?

MISS MERLE

PAPA BOIS, PAPA BOIS
WHAT YOU COOK TODAY?

PAPA BOIS

CRICKET LEG AND *BOIS BANDÉ.*

M. CRAPAUD

PAPA BOIS, PAPA BOIS,
WHAT YOU COOK TODAY?

PAPA BOIS

Un gros crapaud et un gibier.
I'm boiling up some green fig
in this black kerosene tin;
it keeps me sinewy and big,
not too big, not too thin.
The grass grows from my heart,
my eyelids are butterflies,

my legs are two old twigs
one fall could break apart,
like dying coals my eyes.
A calabash my vessel,
this bush salad I eat,
rosemary, watercrestle,
but no meat, boy, no meat.
In mercy we begin,
in mercy may we end;
love every living thing,
the *tête-chien* in his spotted skin.
In spite of his paralyzing sting
the snake is still my friend.
Parsley, celery, aloes,
bitter-herb, *agroment* too;
pepper and peas and eddoes
all bubble in my stew.
You are the child of nature.
This island is your own.
Protect each living creature,
love every bush and stone.
But when you work for the Planter
make sure you don't get vex,
be careful how you answer,
the Planter-man has tricks.
Go on, then, and good luck.

        [*Interior.* PROSPÈRE *'s cabaret. Night.*]

M. CRAPAUD

From *bitation* they come
from L'Ouverte and where from?
Bamboo, fife, goatskin drum,
from Canaries, from Diamond,
as if they were summoned
to dance in the street
and make children afraid
of their mad masquerade,
rolling *La Peau Cabrite*,
dancing for cash
in their *paille banane* trash.

IMPS

Voyez de l'eau ba moin
Moin ka brulé.
SEE HOW I TURNING, TURNING
I HOT YES, I BURNING, BURNING

M. CRAPAUD

Is so every year
in sweet Soufrière,
music making it hotter;
stop at Café Prospère
for a rum without water
or an ice-cold beer.
Hear the drum, hear the fife,

make the best of your life.
Jouez, garçon, jouez,
is Boxing Day today,
moko jumbie so high
like they scraping the sky.

IMPS

Voyez de l'eau ba moin
Moin ka brulé!
Voyez de l'eau ba moin
Moin ka brulé.
THROW WATER ON ME
I'M BURNING

NARRATOR

The three musicians knew him,
from Piaille to Saltibus.
They sang his *chanson* to him
inside a country bus.
They were going to a *marron*
at old Prospère's café.
He had booked them to play on
Après Noel, Boxing Day.
But now, in the boy's features,
they saw such innocence,
that smiling on the creatures

he could dissolve their sins.

So they pleaded:

MISS MERLE

[*Singing.*]

MOON-CHILD, COME LIVE WITH ME
SUN-CHILD, COME LIVE WITH ME
EARTH-CHILD, COME LIVE WITH ME
GOD'S CHILD, WE ALL CAN BE

M. CRAPAUD, M. CRICHETTE

EACH AND EVERY ONE
WE'VE GOT TO LIVE TOGETHER
OUT THERE IN THE FIELDS
AND ALL OVER THE LAND
BROTHERS UNDER THE SUN
CHILDREN SEE THE LIGHT
IT'S ALWAYS AROUND
EVEN AT NIGHT . . .

M. CRICHETTE

MOON-CHILD, COME LIVE WITH ME

M. CRAPAUD

SUN-CHILD, COME LIVE WITH ME
ALL OVER THE EARTH, CHILD

IMPS

COME LIVE WITH ME

MISS MERLE

GOD'S CHILD WE ALL CAN BE

IMPS

LA LA LA LA LA LA
LA LA LA LA LA LA
LA LA LA LA LA LA
LA LA LA LA

[*Country music. Wild banjo.* BETTY FAY *flits onstage.*]

M. CRAPAUD

SHE WAS THE WATCHMAN'S DAUGHTER
HER NAME WAS BETTY FAY
A LITTLE SCARED OF WATER
SHE HID MOST OF THE DAY

BUT AT NIGHT SHE GREW BOLDER
HER BODY GLOWED FROM FAR
TI-JEAN LIKED THAT, HE TOLD HER
"YOU'RE NO FIREFLY, YOU'RE A STAR!"

BETTY FAY

SHE SAID, I'LL BE YOUR DIVA
YOUR INCANDESCENT PEARL

M. CRAPAUD

HE WANTED TO BELIEVE HER
SO SHE BECAME HIS GIRL
HER WAYS WERE VERY WINNING
SHE WAS HIS DEAREST FRIEND
BRIGHT FROM THE BEGINNING
AND BRIGHTER AT THE END

MISS MERLE

SOMETIMES AT HARVEST TIME, YOU SEE
HIGH FIRE AND HELLISH HAZE
FROM *USINE* AND FROM FACTORY
THE SPARK IS BETTY FAY'S

M. CRAPAUD

THE LABOURERS WERE DISSATISFIED
WORKING IN THAT PLACE
THE PLANTER TOOK AWAY THEIR PRIDE
THEIR STRENGTH, THEIR SENSE, THEIR RACE

NARRATOR

Tenebrous pods of cocoa
grew under flaming boughs,
too young to be a worker
he did jobs round the house.

The pods were red, gold, ochre,
they raked and danced the beans;
he loved to steal the cocoa,
what happiness was Ti-Jean's!

The memory of his brothers
was a pain that never healed,
carrying water to the workers,
burning in the hot cane field.
    [THE GOAT *bleats and bleats.* TI-JEAN: *"Shut up!"*]
The same as his two brothers
tired of its stubborn throat,
instead of taking orders
he eunuchised the goat.
    [THE GOAT *'s bleating changes.*]
At an ornate mahogany
table, the boy would sit
as the white man heaped money
that seemed infinite;
then when his job was done
and the tied bags out of reach,
he crept to a parapet
that overlooked the beach
with its embroidered ocean,
then dropped with a hawk's plummet
and its widening motion.

Every infernal dusk
this black-winged, ragged shape
rose from the day's dry dust
with its slow, flapping cape;
a shape that drifted soaring
above the golden sea.
It was the Planter, touring
his widening property;
his empire's expansion
increasing stone by stone,
yet the Lord of the Mansion
ate every night alone.

Do you know what his menu
at midnight would comprise
in that spider-webbed venue?
Crab claws and frog's eyes,
caterpillar, crayfish, lizard,
black-pudding, cockroach, souse,
onion, and chicken gizzard,
moss, *manicou*, field mouse;
the mounds of food were hellish
and Ti-Jean watched him dine,
joylessly, without relish,
sipping disconsolate wine.

The canes at night made a huge noise,
star-sparks lit the cane-sea,
and the canes threshed like prisoners
struggling to pull free.
The master had a mission
in Soufrière, after dinner,
a calypso competition
where he would be the winner.
The Planter was a hot boy,
the way the Devil was;
he loved his carnival, to enjoy
a fête like all of us.

Rats leave a sinking ship, so
do creatures a forest fire.
Harvest time brings calypso,
the music getting higher.

The lyrics getting harder,
the singers have no option,
like this khaki-voiced cicada,
than to condemn corruption.

M. CRAPAUD

And now, for Boxing Night in Soufrière.
We present *compère* Crichette, the calypsonian,
and Mr. Cricket is coming to knock you out—Yeah!

BACKUP GIRLS

MONEY PASS
MONEY PASS
UNDER DE TABLE
PEOPLE GETTING RICH FAST
BUT ME, I AIN'T ABLE

[*A dance: "Bribery."*]

M. CRICHETTE

SO MUCH HOTEL GOING UP
SO MUCH O' CONDO
DEVELOPMENT LIKE IT CAN'T STOP
WHAT CAN POOR PEOPLE DO?

M. CRAPAUD

GET A JOB AS WAITER AND CRAPAUD MAID
ON THE NEW PLANTATION
INVESTMENT FROM FOREIGN AID
GOD HELP MY NATION

BACKUP GIRLS

MONEY PASS
MONEY PASS
UNDER DE TABLE
PEOPLE GETTING RICH FAST
BUT ME, I AIN'T ABLE

M. CRICHETTE

WHEN IT COME TO GRABBING LAND
MAN DOES BE WICKED
BUT ME, I CAN'T UNDERSTAND
I AM JUST A CRICKET

EVERYWHERE I LOOK I SEE
A MINI-MIAMI
TOO MUCH IN THIS SMALL COUNTRY
DOES REALLY ALARM ME

BACKUP GIRLS

MONEY PASS
MONEY PASS
UNDER DE TABLE
PEOPLE GETTING RICH FAST
BUT ME, I AIN'T ABLE

M. CRICHETTE

LET US TAKE A LESSON FROM
TI-JEAN AND HIS BROTHERS
HOW HIGH-RISES GOING TO COME
FROM LAND THAT WAS HIS MOTHER'S

MORE AND MORE NEGOTIATION
LEAVING POOR PEOPLE STRANDED

THEY GO SELL OUT MY POOR NATION
UNLESS JUSTICE IS DEMANDED

BACKUP GIRLS

MONEY PASS
MONEY PASS
UNDER DE TABLE
PEOPLE GETTING RICH FAST
BUT ME, I AIN'T ABLE

M. CRAPAUD

Such disobedience borders
on the edge of anarchy,
but Ti-Jean took no orders
from red men in khaki.
He saw that their devotion
was only there for hire,
and he and the Firefly caught the ocean
of waving cane on fire.
The sale of land was booming
but so was knavery,
and what the boy saw looming
was a second slavery.

> [*Drumming. Dancers—
> a cane fire.*]

BETTY FAY

I can help you, Ti-Jean.
You have the kerosene?

TI-JEAN

Yes, proceed.

BETTY FAY

Put it on my backside.
It'll catch the canes on fire.

> [*Sound of crackling fire, bursts of bamboo,*
> *screams, shouts, drumming.*]

TI-JEAN
[*Singing.*]
THE MAN SAY BURN, BURN, BURN DE CANE!

LABOURERS

BURN, BURN, BURN DE CANE!

TI-JEAN

YOU TIRED WORK FOR THE MAN IN VAIN!

LABOURERS

BURN, BURN, BURN DE CANE!

TI-JEAN

TOO MUCH MISERY, TOO MUCH PAIN!

LABOURERS

BURN, BURN, BURN DE CANE!

TI-JEAN

NO MORE SLAVERY AGAIN!
THE MAN SAY BURN, BURN, BURN DE CANE!

LABOURERS

BURN, BURN, BURN DE CANE!

TI-JEAN

YOU TIRED WORK FOR THE MAN IN VAIN!

LABOURERS

BURN, BURN, BURN DE CANE!

TI-JEAN

TOO MUCH MISERY, TOO MUCH PAIN!

LABOURERS

BURN, BURN, BURN DE CANE!

NARRATOR

Was this so unexpected?
The Devil loves a fire,
and wasn't this holocaust the spread
of his immense empire?

M. CRAPAUD

And all night the night burned,
turning on its spit,
the stars burning like holes,
when the Planter, dressed like the Devil, returned,
singing his songs of lost souls.

THE PLANTER
[*Singing.*]

DOWN DEEP IN HELL, WHERE IT BLACK LIKE INK
WHERE DE OIL DOES BOIL AND THE SULPHUR
    STINK
IT AIN'T HAVE NO ICE, NO REFRIGERATOR
IF YOU WANT WATER, AND YOU ASK THE
    WAITER
HE GO BRING BRIMSTONE WITH A SALTPETRE
    CHASER
WHILE THE DEVIL'S BAWLING

BACKUP GIRLS

FIRE ONE!

FIRE ONE! FIRE ONE TILL THE PLACE BURN DOWN!

FIRE ONE! . . .

[*Noise—distant. Screams. The estate on fire.*]

THE PLANTER

SO WHEN PEOPLE BAWLING HOW THE DEVIL BAD

IT DOES GET ME VEX, IT DOES MAKE ME SAD

CAUSE TO LIVE LIKE A DRAGON ONLY BELCHING
  SMOKE

WHEN YOU FEELING FOR A FLAGON IS A HELL OF
  A JOKE

WHEN YOUR ICE IS COALS, AND YOUR STRAW IS A
  POKER

WHILE YOUR BACKUP BAWLING

BACKUP GIRLS

FIRE ONE!

FIRE ONE! FIRE ONE TILL THE PLACE BURN DOWN!

FIRE ONE! . . .

THE PLANTER

SINCE I PITCH LIKE A METEOR TO MY BURNING
  SHAME

THE LORD FALL-DOWN WAS MY GIVEN NAME

SO I SINGING CALYPSO TO REGAIN MY FAME
AS THE SPARKS FLY UPWARD, MY ONLY AIM
IS THAT STARRY CROWN, SO I SINGING ME SOCA
WHILE THE DEVIL'S BAWLING

BACKUP GIRLS

FIRE ONE!
FIRE ONE! FIRE ONE TILL THE PLACE BURN DOWN!
FIRE ONE!

THE PLANTER

"When I was the Son of the Morning, when I was the Prince of Light." Oh, to hell with that! You lose a job, you lose a job!

BETTY FAY

Let me guide you home, boss.

THE PLANTER

Get out of my way, you burning backside! I'm the Prince of Darkness and I won't brook interruption! To hell with dependence and secondary lieutenancy! I had a host of burnished helmets once and a forest of soldiery waiting on my cough, on my very belch! Yet we were one light once, the Old Man and I. I had a love of God once, but He fired me!

[*Singing.*]
AND SO I FELL FOR FORTY YEARS
PASSING THE STARS IN THE ENDLESS PIT!
You nearly scared me. How long you been hiding there? I
won, of course. Best costume! Just bribed the judges. Some-
how I liked you, little man. You have courage. Well now, it's
time to go home.

TI-JEAN

You can't go home, sir.

THE PLANTER

Why not?

TI-JEAN

You'll see.

[*A blaze lightens the sky.*]

THE PLANTER

I think I'll be going up to the house. Why don't you come
in? It's suddenly got so bright. Is that fire?

TI-JEAN

Looks like fire, yes.

THE PLANTER

Well, what do you think it is, my little friend?

TI-JEAN

I think it's your house.

THE PLANTER

I don't understand.

TI-JEAN

Have a drink. In fact, I'm pretty certain it's your home. I left a few things on fire in it from some kerosene I went to buy for my mother.

THE PLANTER
[*Roaring.*]

It's the nicest house I had, boy!

TI-JEAN

My mother lost two sons, she didn't get vex.

THE PLANTER

What the hell do you think I care about your mother, boy? The poor withered fool who thinks it's holy to be poor, who scraped her knees to the knuckle praying to an old beard who's been deaf since time began? Or your two damned fools of brothers, the man of strength and the rhetorician? Come! Filambo! Azaz! Cacaret! You've burnt property that belongs to me.

[*Exterior. The sky brightens above the fire.*
Bats and winged creatures cross it.]

TI-JEAN

Come on, sir, play fair!

THE PLANTER

Who with the Devil tries to play fair
weaves the net of his own despair.

TI-JEAN

You owe me, sir. You vex!

THE PLANTER

I've been watching you, Ti-Jean, you little nowhere nigger!
You little squirt, you hackneyed cough between two immor-
talities, who do you think you are? You're dirt, and that's
where you'll be when I'm finished with you. Burn my house,
my receipts, all my papers, all my bloody triumphs.

[THE BOLOM *crawls up from a fissure in the earth.*]

TI-JEAN

Does your master sound vexed to you? Answer me, Bolom!

THE BOLOM

Master, be fair!

THE PLANTER

Look in your house, boy, up there in Bouton, where your
mother is dying!

[*Exterior.* THE MOTHER's *house.*]

TI-JEAN

Maman!

THE MOTHER

[*Singing.*]

TO THE DOOR OF BREATH YOU GAVE THE KEY
THANK YOU, LORD
THE DOOR IS OPEN AND I STEP FREE
AMEN, LORD
CLOUD AFTER CLOUD LIKE A SILVER STAIR
MY LOVED ONES WAITING TO GREET ME THERE
WITH THEIR SILENT FACES AND STARLIT HAIR
AMEN, LORD

[*A golden tree, near the house, drops its leaves like coins.*]

NARRATOR

In the high mountain mist,
as the long day was done,
the sky unclenched its fist
and kept one coin, the sun,
and then that brazen tree
turned its leaves into coins

called the *gommier maudit*.
They fell increasingly
into earth's waiting loins.
The debt was being paid
that her three sons had made.

TI-JEAN

Maman!

THE PLANTER

She cannot hear you, child. Now can you still sing?

THE BOLOM

Ask him for my life! O God, I want all this to happen to me!

TI-JEAN

Is life you want, child? You don't see what it bring?

THE BOLOM

Yes, yes, Ti-Jean, life!

TI-JEAN

Don't blame me when you suffering.

THE PLANTER

Is what you want life? Life and its one ending.

THE BOLOM

Yes, life!

[*Sounds. The ground in convulsions.* THE BOLOM *is born.*
Throbbing bass. Heartbeat.]

[*Being born.*]

I AM BORN, I SHALL DIE! I AM BORN, I SHALL DIE!
OH THE WONDER AND PRIDE OF IT! I SHALL
BE MAN!

WASHERWOMEN

Sing, Ti-Jean, sing!
Show him you could win!
Sing, Ti-Jean . . . listen,
all around you nature
still singing.

TI-JEAN

[*Singing.*]

TO THE DOOR OF BREATH YOU GAVE THE KEY
THANK YOU, LORD
THE DOOR IS OPEN AND I STEP FREE
AMEN, LORD
CLOUD AFTER CLOUD LIKE A SILVER STAIR
MY LOVED ONES WAITING TO GREET ME THERE

WITH THEIR SILENT FACES AND STARLIT HAIR
AMEN, LORD
>[*Exterior. Volcano.* THE PLANTER *weeps.*
>*A tear, then tears singe his hot face.*]

THE PLANTER

WHAT IS THIS COOLING MY FACE?
TEARS! TEARS!
YOU HAVE WON, TI-JEAN!

WASHERWOMEN

TI-JEAN, YOU HAVE WON!
>[*The cathedral bell tolls.*]

NARRATOR

As slowly as a teardrop
the cathedral tolls,
praying that evil stop,
praying for our lost souls;
slow, down the Planter's cheek,
in shame for his lost world,
in charity, not weak,
his sorrow slides, empearled.
No more money under the table
or ripping off the poor.
The moral of this fable
is—Innocence is Power.

Soft-spoken as the serpent
in the first garden, who
mamaguyed our first parent
with fruit he led him to.
That was the golden apple,
acid at first, then sweet,
the snake, erect and supple,
bade simple Adam eat,
and from that bite there flowered
the sorrow of the world,
till he was overpowered
and from high heaven hurled.

What comet dug this crater,
if not the shooting star,
who challenged his Creator,
the rebel, Lucifer?
With sparks of stars behind him,
his path scorching the air,
in smoke and ash you'll find him,
he fell in Soufrière.
And where he fell the warning
of lava horns both rise
to show the Son of Morning
how he lost paradise.

THE PLANTER

Farewell, little fool! Come, then, my legions! My band!
Stretch your wings and soar, pass over the fields
like the last shadow of night, imps, devils, bats!
Soleil-la! Soleil-la!
The sun, the sun!

[*Exits.*]

NARRATOR

His screech of rage grew higher,
it turned their blood to frost;
he leapt into the fire
and paradise was lost;
the trees were singed around him,
the springs began to boil,
he felt white smoke surround him
and sank into the soil.

TI-JEAN

Come then, Bolom, my new little brother,
and bless you creatures.
Ti-Jean must go on.
Here's a bundle of sticks that old wisdom
has forgotten. Together they are strong,
apart they are all rotten.

[PAPA BOIS *appears, holding a snake*
which stings him. He falls.]

NARRATOR

As for that bearded hermit
who walked between the leaves,
whose voice the falls inherit,
for whom the blackbird grieves.
A serpent stung him when he passed,
but with all that, he was able
to make the forest last.
He slid into his fable,
he fades into the past,
as water drinks a stone
or a pool its own reflection,
with a deep-rooted groan,
Papa Bois was gone.

Around his mother's head, turned white,
an apparition grows,
as, at an altar, rays of light
revolve around a rose,
as in this fable her three sons
pay homage to her glory,
as you have heard it at least once,
this simple Creole story.
Let all the lilies in the grass,
if we could hear their voices,
sing out the hallelujahs
in which a bird rejoices.

MISS MERLE

[*Singing.*]

WHO MAKE THE DEVIL CRY?

WASHERWOMEN

TI-JEAN!

MISS MERLE

BRING WATER TO HIS EYE?

WASHERWOMEN

TI-JEAN

MISS MERLE

WHOSE STORY NEVER DIE?

WASHERWOMEN

TI-JEAN

M. CRAPAUD

AND HE SAILING WITH THE MOON

NARRATOR

The immortelle's flameless fire
along the mountain ranges
still runs; cherish it before
the whole island changes

before music as custom
like the dew disappears,
fading like the goatskin drum
that brought a mother's tears

When smoke roils from the crater
of the volcano's rim,
we know that every creature
singing remembers him,
that in the full moon's mirror
when the moon plays its tricks,
there is a boy, a minor,
carrying a bunch of sticks;
a boy with sticks who's able
to bear them on his back;
a boy who is our fable.
Messieurs, bon-soir, crik-crak.
                    [*Music.*]

M. CRAPAUD

WHO CHALLENGE PAPA BOIS?

WASHERWOMEN

TI-JEAN!

MISS MERLE

WHO LAUGH AT LUCIFER?

WASHERWOMEN

TI-JEAN!

MISS MERLE

WHO SEE YOU WHEN YOU SUFFER?

WASHERWOMEN

TI-JEAN!

M. CRAPAUD

AND HE SAILING WITH THE MOON

M. CRICHETTE

AND ALL THE COUNTRY CHILDREN
SINGING THIS TUNE

M. CRAPAUD

NOW THE *GENS-GAGÉ* WALKING
MAMAN DE L'EAU START TO SWIM
LITTLE BOLOM START TALKING
BUT YOU CAN'T TALK BACK TO HIM
YOU CAN'T TALK BACK TO HIM
NOW THE LOUPGAROU HIDING
IN THE USUAL PLACE
WHEN THE SMALL OWL START BRIGHTENING
THE TWO MOONS IN HER FACE

WASHERWOMEN

THE TWO MOONS IN HER FACE

M. CRICHETTE

WHO MAKES THE CRICKET SING?

WASHERWOMEN

TI-JEAN!

M. CRAPAUD

WHO CROWN THE CRAPAUD KING?

WASHERWOMEN

TI-JEAN!

M. CRAPAUD

AND HE HAPPY AS THE MOON
AND ALL THE COUNTRY CHILDREN
SINGING THIS TUNE

WASHERWOMEN

LA LA LA LA LA LA
LA LA
LA LA LA LA LA LA
LA LA

NARRATOR, WASHERWOMEN, CREATURES

Gloria chaud	*A hot Gloria*
Gloria frette	*A cold Gloria*
Gloria pour	*A Gloria for*
Toute ça nous connaître	*Everything we know*
Gloria pour botay, la comette	*Gloria for botay, la comette*
Gloria Choiseul	*Gloria Choiseul*
Gloria Soufrière	*Gloria Soufrière*
Gloria plus belle	*Gloria plus belle*
Pour tout ça nous ka weh	*In everything we see*
Gloria	*In everything we hear*
Gloria	*Gloria*
Gloria	*Gloria*

END

Printed in the USA
CPSIA information can be obtained
at www.ICGtesting.com
LVHW091146150724
785511LV00005B/580